Wedding
Planner

She said Yes

Wedding Contacts

Caterer

Name
_____

Website
_____

Address
_____

Phone
_____

Email
_____

Notes
_____

_____

Name
_____

Website
_____

Address
_____

Phone
_____

Email
_____

Notes
_____

_____

Ceremony venue

Name
_____

Website
_____

Address
_____

Phone
_____

Email
_____

Notes
_____

_____

Name
_____

Website
_____

Address
_____

Phone
_____

Email
_____

Notes
_____

_____

Wedding Contacts

Wedding planner

Name _____

Website _____

Address _____

Phone _____

Email _____

Notes _____

_____

Name _____

Website _____

Address _____

Phone _____

Email _____

Notes _____

_____

Reception venue

Name _____

Website _____

Address _____

Phone _____

Email _____

Notes _____

_____

Name _____

Website _____

Address _____

Phone _____

Email _____

Notes _____

_____

Wedding Contacts

Cake baker

Name

Website

Address

Phone

Email

Notes

Name

Website

Address

Phone

Email

Notes

Rehearsal dinner venue

Name

Website

Address

Phone

Email

Notes

Name

Website

Address

Phone

Email

Notes

Wedding Contacts

Makeup artist

Name

Website

Address

Phone

Email

Notes

Name

Website

Address

Phone

Email

Notes

Hair stylist

Name

Website

Address

Phone

Email

Notes

Name

Website

Address

Phone

Email

Notes

Wedding Contacts

Dress designer/dress shop

Name

Website

Address

Phone

Email

Notes

Name

Website

Address

Phone

Email

Notes

Of ciant

Name

Website

Address

Phone

Email

Notes

Name

Website

Address

Phone

Email

Notes

Wedding Contacts

Hotel for out of town guests

Name

Website

Address

Phone

Email

Notes

Name

Website

Address

Phone

Email

Notes

Ceremony venue

Name

Website

Address

Phone

Email

Notes

Name

Website

Address

Phone

Email

Notes

Wedding Contacts

Photographer

Name
_____

Website
_____

Address
_____

Phone
_____

Email
_____

Notes
_____

_____

Name
_____

Website
_____

Address
_____

Phone
_____

Email
_____

Notes
_____

_____

Videographer

Name
_____

Website
_____

Address
_____

Phone
_____

Email
_____

Notes
_____

_____

Name
_____

Website
_____

Address
_____

Phone
_____

Email
_____

Notes
_____

_____

Wedding Contacts

Rental company

Name

Website

Address

Phone

Email

Notes

Name

Website

Address

Phone

Email

Notes

DJ / band

Name

Website

Address

Phone

Email

Notes

Name

Website

Address

Phone

Email

Notes

Wedding Contacts

Stationery designer

Name
_____

Website
_____

Address
_____

Phone
_____

Email
_____

Notes
_____

_____

Name
_____

Website
_____

Address
_____

Phone
_____

Email
_____

Notes
_____

_____

Transportation

Name
_____

Website
_____

Address
_____

Phone
_____

Email
_____

Notes
_____

_____

Name
_____

Website
_____

Address
_____

Phone
_____

Email
_____

Notes
_____

_____

Wedding Contacts

Florist

Name
_____

Website
_____

Address
_____

Phone
_____

Email
_____

Notes
_____

Name
_____

Website
_____

Address
_____

Phone
_____

Email
_____

Notes
_____

Welcome party venue

Name
_____

Website
_____

Address
_____

Phone
_____

Email
_____

Notes
_____

Name
_____

Website
_____

Address
_____

Phone
_____

Email
_____

Notes
_____

Wedding Contacts

Other

Name
_____

Website
_____

Address
_____

Phone
_____

Email
_____

Notes
_____

_____

Name
_____

Website
_____

Address
_____

Phone
_____

Email
_____

Notes
_____

_____

Name
_____

Website
_____

Address
_____

Phone
_____

Email
_____

Notes
_____

_____

Name
_____

Website
_____

Address
_____

Phone
_____

Email
_____

Notes
_____

_____

Wedding Contacts

Other

Name

Website

Address

Phone

Email

Notes

Name

Website

Address

Phone

Email

Notes

Name

Website

Address

Phone

Email

Notes

Name

Website

Address

Phone

Email

Notes

Wedding Guest List

Name	Address	Phone

Wedding Guest List

Reply Recived (y/n)	Invited #	Attending #	Not Attending

Wedding Guest List

Name	Address	Phone

Wedding Guest List

Reply Recived (y/n)	Invited #	Attending #	Not Attending

Wedding Guest List

Name	Address	Phone

Wedding Guest List

Reply Recived (y/n)	Invited #	Attending #	Not Attending

Wedding Gift Tracker

Gift	Gift Description	Gift By	Thank -You Card Sent?
			☐
			☐
			☐
			☐
			☐
			☐
			☐
			☐
			☐
			☐
			☐
			☐
			☐
			☐
			☐
			☐
			☐
			☐
			☐
			☐
			☐
			☐
			☐
			☐
			☐
			☐
			☐

Wedding Budget

Item / Service	Budgeted	Vendor Est.	Spent
PLANNING			
WEDDING BINDER			
WEDDING COORDINATOR / PLANNER			
WEDDING MAGAZINES			
TOTAL:			
VIDEO & PHOTOGRAPHY			
ENGAGEMENT PHOTO SHOOT			
WEDDING PHOTO SHOOT			
WEDDING VIDEOGRAPHY			
PRINTED PHOTOS FOR US			
PHOTOS FOR THANK-YOU CARDS			
PHOTO ALBUMS FOR US			
PHOTO ALBUMS FOR OUR PARENTS			
TOTAL:			
RINGS			
ENGAGEMENT RING			
BRIDE'S RING			
GROOM'S RING			
TOTAL:			
GROOM'S ATTIRE			
SUIT OR TUXEDO			
TIE OR BOW-TIE			
SHOES			

Wedding Budget

Item / Service	Budgeted	Vendor Est.	Spent
Groom's Attire			
Accessories			
Other			
Total:			
Bride's Attire			
Wedding Dress 1			
Wedding Dress 2			
Headpiece / Veil			
Jewelery			
Shoes			
Lingerie			
Makeup			
Hairstyle			
Manicure and Pedicure			
Total:			
STATIONERY			
Save The Date Cards			
Wedding Invitations			
Thank-You Cards			
Seating Plan Display			
Postage			
Ceremony Program			
Menu Cards			
Place Cards			
Other			
Total:			

Wedding Budget

Item / Service	Budgeted	Vendor Est.	Spent
FLOLAR			
BRIDAL BOUQUET			
GROOM'S BOUTONNIERES			
FLOWER GIRL PETALS			
BRIDESMAIDS BOUQUET			
GROOMSMEN BOUTONNIERES			
RING BEARER BOUTONNIERES			
TABLE ARRANGEMENTS			
DELIVERY AND SET-UP			
CORSAGES			
TOTAL:			
GIFTS AND FAVORS			
BRIDESMAID GIFTS			
GROOMSMEN GIFTS			
FLOWER GIRL GIFTS			
OTHER			
TOTAL:			
CEREMONY			
REHEARSAL FEE			
VENUE / CHURCH FEE			
RING PILLOW			
CANDLES			
DJ / MUSICIAN			
POST-CEREMONY FAVORS			
MARRIAGE LICENSE			
OFFICIANT FEE /DONATION			
TOTAL:			

Wedding Budget

Item / Service	Budgeted	Vendor Est.	Spent
TRANSPORTATION			
CAR RENTAL			
TRANSPORTATION FOR OUT OF TOWN GUESTS			
PARKING			
CAR DECORATIONS			
FUEL			
CAR CLEANING			
TAXI SERVICE			
TOTAL:			
RECEPTION			
VENUE RENTAL			
MEAL			
LIQUOR AND BEVERAGES			
CAKE			
DJ AND ENTERTAINMENT			
WEDDING FAVORS			
INSURANCE			
CENTERPIECES			
DECORATIONS			
OTHER RENTALS			
TABLES AND CHAIRS			
SERVICE			
OTHER			
TOTAL:			

Wedding Budget

Item / Service	Budgeted	Vendor Est.	Spent

My Wedding Songs

Artist	Song Title	Song Length

Reception Ideas

Reception Site _____   Phone # _____

Address _____

Contact Person _____   Email _____

Guests # _____   Tables # _____

Item	Cost
Food Ideas	
Drinks	
Total	

Reception Ideas

Reception Site		Phone #	
Address			
Contact Person		Email	
Guests #		Tables #	

Item	Cost
Decorations	
Music	
Photography	
Total	

The CAKE

Bakery _____   Phone # _____

Address _____

Contact Person _____   Email _____

Website : _____

My wedding cake will be

_____

_____

_____

Picture cake

Costs

Cake _____

Slab Cake _____

Delivery _____

Other _____

Total _____

Notes

_____

_____

_____

Wedding Table Plan

Top Table

Table 1

1 _____
2 _____
3 _____
4 _____
5 _____
6 _____
7 _____
8 _____
9 _____
10 _____

Table 2

1 _____
2 _____
3 _____
4 _____
5 _____
6 _____
7 _____
8 _____
9 _____
10 _____

Table 3

1 _____
2 _____
3 _____
4 _____
5 _____
6 _____
7 _____
8 _____
9 _____
10 _____

Table 4

1 _____
2 _____
3 _____
4 _____
5 _____
6 _____
7 _____
8 _____
9 _____
10 _____

Table 5

1 _____
2 _____
3 _____
4 _____
5 _____
6 _____
7 _____
8 _____
9 _____
10 _____

Wedding Table Plan

Table 6
1 _____
2 _____
3 _____
4 _____
5 _____
6 _____
7 _____
8 _____
9 _____
10 _____

Table 7
1 _____
2 _____
3 _____
4 _____
5 _____
6 _____
7 _____
8 _____
9 _____
10 _____

Table 8
1 _____
2 _____
3 _____
4 _____
5 _____
6 _____
7 _____
8 _____
9 _____
10 _____

Table 9
1 _____
2 _____
3 _____
4 _____
5 _____
6 _____
7 _____
8 _____
9 _____
10 _____

Table 10
1 _____
2 _____
3 _____
4 _____
5 _____
6 _____
7 _____
8 _____
9 _____
10 _____

Table 11
1 _____
2 _____
3 _____
4 _____
5 _____
6 _____
7 _____
8 _____
9 _____
10 _____

Notes :
_____
_____
_____
_____

Bachelorette party planner

Bachelorette Party Planner

Date and Time

Venue

Contact Person

Website

Phone #1

Phone #2

Email

Address

Theme

Flowers & decor

Shopping list

- [ ] _____
- [ ] _____
- [ ] _____
- [ ] _____
- [ ] _____
- [ ] _____
- [ ] _____
- [ ] _____
- [ ] _____

Food & Drinks

Notes

_____

_____

Favors

_____

_____

Bachelorette Party Guest List

Guest Name	Email	RSVP	Food / Beverages Brought

Bachelorette Party Schedule

Time	Task or Activity	Notes

Bachelorette Party Gift Tracker

Gift	Gift Description	Gift By	Thank -You Card Sent?
			☐
			☐
			☐
			☐
			☐
			☐
			☐
			☐
			☐
			☐
			☐
			☐
			☐
			☐
			☐
			☐
			☐
			☐
			☐
			☐
			☐
			☐
			☐
			☐
			☐
			☐
			☐
			☐

Bachelorette Party Timeline

When ?	To-Do	Notes	Done
			☐
			☐
			☐
			☐
			☐
			☐
			☐
			☐
			☐
			☐
			☐
			☐
			☐
			☐
			☐
			☐
			☐
			☐
			☐
			☐
			☐
			☐
			☐
			☐
			☐
			☐

Bachelorette Party Shopping List

- [ ] _____
- [ ] _____
- [ ] _____
- [ ] _____
- [ ] _____
- [ ] _____
- [ ] _____
- [ ] _____
- [ ] _____
- [ ] _____
- [ ] _____
- [ ] _____
- [ ] _____
- [ ] _____
- [ ] _____
- [ ] _____
- [ ] _____
- [ ] _____
- [ ] _____

- [ ] _____
- [ ] _____
- [ ] _____
- [ ] _____
- [ ] _____
- [ ] _____
- [ ] _____
- [ ] _____
- [ ] _____
- [ ] _____
- [ ] _____
- [ ] _____
- [ ] _____
- [ ] _____
- [ ] _____
- [ ] _____
- [ ] _____
- [ ] _____
- [ ] _____

Bachelorette Party Notes

Bachelorette Party Menu

Menu

Snacks & Appetizers:

_____

_____

_____

_____

_____

_____

_____

Main Food:

_____

_____

_____

_____

_____

_____

_____

Grocery list

☐ _____

☐ _____

☐ _____

☐ _____

☐ _____

☐ _____

☐ _____

☐ _____

☐ _____

☐ _____

☐ _____

☐ _____

☐ _____

☐ _____

☐ _____

☐ _____

☐ _____

☐ _____

☐ _____

☐ _____

Bachelorette Party Menu

Drinks:
_____
_____
_____
_____
_____
_____

Cake:
_____
_____
_____

Notes:
_____
_____
_____
_____

☐ _____
☐ _____
☐ _____
☐ _____
☐ _____
☐ _____
☐ _____
☐ _____
☐ _____
☐ _____
☐ _____
☐ _____
☐ _____
☐ _____

Bachelorette Party Expenses

Food / Drinks	Budgeted Amt.	Amt. Spent	Notes
Total			
Supplies			
Total			
Entertainment			
Total			

Bridal shower planner

Bridal Shower Schedule

Time	Task or Activity	Notes

Bridal Shower Planner

Date and Time

Venue   Contact Person

Website   Phone #1

Phone #2   Email

Address

Theme

Flowers & Decor

Shopping list

- [ ] _____
- [ ] _____
- [ ] _____
- [ ] _____
- [ ] _____
- [ ] _____
- [ ] _____
- [ ] _____
- [ ] _____

Food & Drinks

Notes

_____
_____
_____

Favors

_____
_____

Bridal Shower Guest List

Guest Name	Email	RSVP	Food / Beverages Brought

Bridal Shower Gift Tracker

Gift	Gift Description	Gift By	Thank -You Card Sent?
			☐
			☐
			☐
			☐
			☐
			☐
			☐
			☐
			☐
			☐
			☐
			☐
			☐
			☐
			☐
			☐
			☐
			☐
			☐
			☐
			☐
			☐
			☐
			☐
			☐
			☐
			☐
			☐

Bridal Shower Timeline

Date. . . . .

When ?	To-Do	Notes	Done
2-3 MONTHS BEFORE	pick a date and		☐
	timepick a venue		☐
	create a guest list		☐
	set a budget		☐
	order invitations		☐
	send a save the		☐
	datedecide theme		☐
MONTH BEFORE1	send invitations		☐
	select		☐
	decorationsbuy favors		☐
	plan the menu		☐
	select activities		☐
	order rentals		☐
	make shopping list		☐
WEEK BEFORE	prepare favors		☐
	purchase drinkscall		☐
	on RSVPsconfirm		☐
	venue and caterer		☐
	buy your gift		☐
	shop for groceries		☐
1 DAY BEFOREONE	prepare food and setup		☐
	decorcharge camera		☐
	confirm plans		☐
	prepare items for activities		☐
THE DAY	keep a list of gift givers		☐
	have fun!		☐
			☐

Bridal Shower Timeline

Date. . . . .

When ?	To-Do	Notes	Done
2-3 MONTHS BEFORE			☐
			☐
			☐
			☐
			☐
			☐
			☐
MONTH BEFORE1			☐
			☐
			☐
			☐
			☐
			☐
			☐
WEEK BEFORE			☐
			☐
			☐
			☐
			☐
			☐
1 DAY BEFOREONE			☐
			☐
			☐
			☐
THE DAY			☐
			☐
			☐

Bridal Shower Shopping List

☐ _____   ☐ _____
☐ _____   ☐ _____
☐ _____   ☐ _____
☐ _____   ☐ _____
☐ _____   ☐ _____
☐ _____   ☐ _____
☐ _____   ☐ _____
☐ _____   ☐ _____
☐ _____   ☐ _____
☐ _____   ☐ _____
☐ _____   ☐ _____
☐ _____   ☐ _____
☐ _____   ☐ _____
☐ _____   ☐ _____
☐ _____   ☐ _____
☐ _____   ☐ _____
☐ _____   ☐ _____
☐ _____   ☐ _____

Bridal Shower Notes

_____
_____
_____
_____
_____
_____
_____
_____
_____
_____
_____
_____
_____
_____
_____
_____
_____
_____
_____
_____

Bridal Shower Menu

Menu

Snacks & Appetizers:

_____

_____

_____

_____

_____

_____

_____

Main Food:

_____

_____

_____

_____

_____

_____

Grocery list

☐ _____

☐ _____

☐ _____

☐ _____

☐ _____

☐ _____

☐ _____

☐ _____

☐ _____

☐ _____

☐ _____

☐ _____

☐ _____

☐ _____

☐ _____

☐ _____

☐ _____

☐ _____

☐ _____

Bridal Shower Menu

Drinks:

_____

_____

_____

_____

_____

_____

Cake:

_____

_____

_____

☐ _____

☐ _____

☐ _____

☐ _____

☐ _____

☐ _____

☐ _____

☐ _____

☐ _____

☐ _____

☐ _____

☐ _____

☐ _____

☐ _____

Notes:

_____

_____

_____

_____

Bridal Shower Expenses

Food / Drinks	Budgeted Amt.	Amt. Spent	Notes
Total			
Supplies			
Total			
Entertainment			
Total			

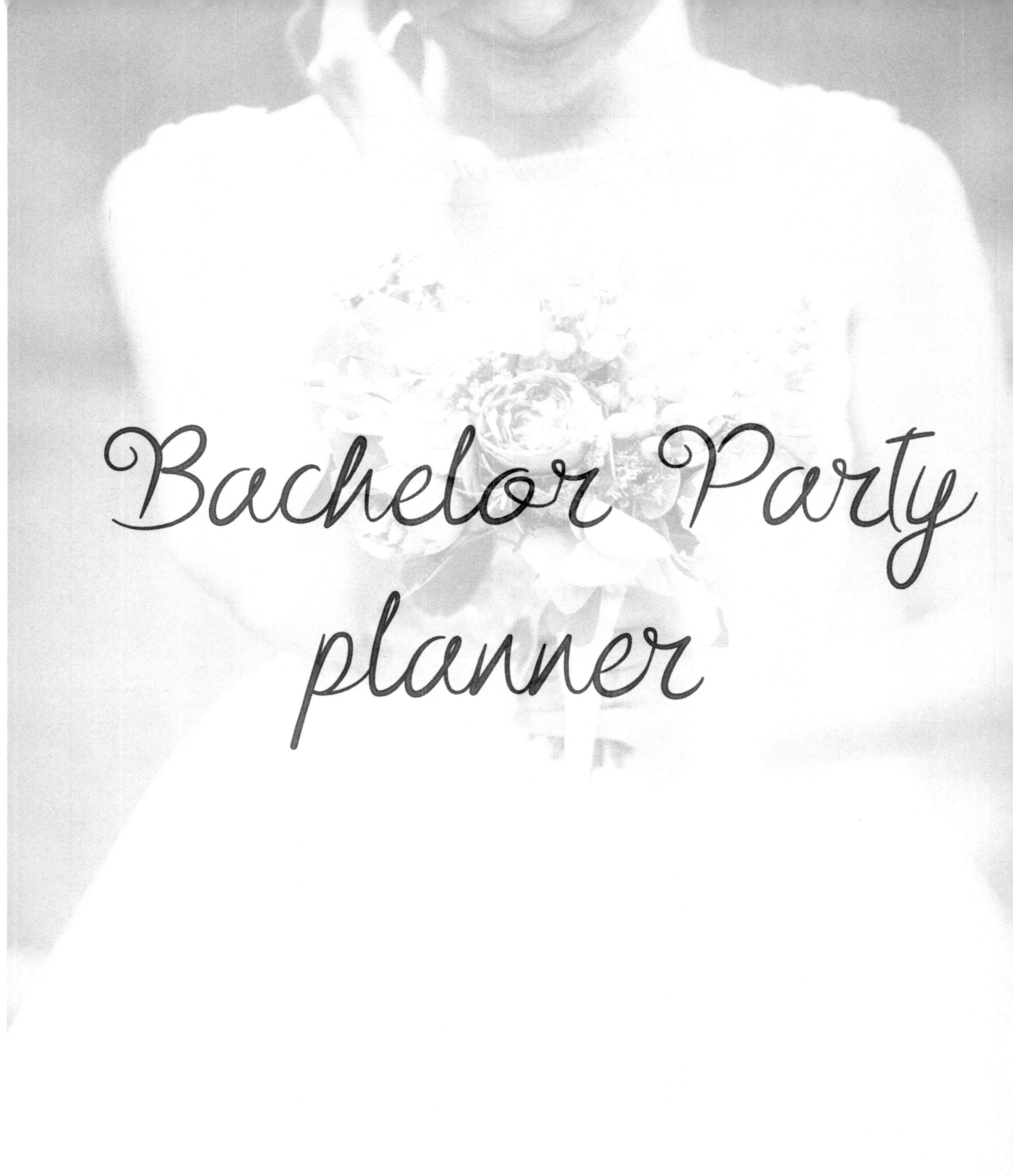

Bachelor Party planner

Bridal Shower Timeline

When ?	To-Do	Notes	Done
			☐
			☐
			☐
			☐
			☐
			☐
			☐
			☐
			☐
			☐
			☐
			☐
			☐
			☐
			☐
			☐
			☐
			☐
			☐
			☐
			☐
			☐
			☐
			☐
			☐
			☐
			☐

Bachelor Party Schedule

Time	Task or Activity	Notes

Bachelor Party Planner

Date and Time _____

Venue _____ Contact Person _____

Website _____ Phone #1 _____

Phone #2 _____ Email _____

Address _____

Theme _____

_____

Flowers & Decor

_____

_____

_____

Food & Drinks

_____

_____

Favors

_____

_____

_____

Shopping list

- [ ] _____
- [ ] _____
- [ ] _____
- [ ] _____
- [ ] _____
- [ ] _____
- [ ] _____
- [ ] _____
- [ ] _____
- [ ] _____
- [ ] _____
- [ ] _____
- [ ] _____
- [ ] _____

Bachelor Party Guest List

Guest Name	Email	RSVP	Food / Beverages Brought

Bachelor Party Gift Tracker

Gift	Gift Description	Gift By	Thank -You Card Sent?
			☐
			☐
			☐
			☐
			☐
			☐
			☐
			☐
			☐
			☐
			☐
			☐
			☐
			☐
			☐
			☐
			☐
			☐
			☐
			☐
			☐
			☐
			☐
			☐
			☐
			☐
			☐
			☐

Bachelor Party Shopping List

- [ ] _____
- [ ] _____
- [ ] _____
- [ ] _____
- [ ] _____
- [ ] _____
- [ ] _____
- [ ] _____
- [ ] _____
- [ ] _____
- [ ] _____
- [ ] _____
- [ ] _____
- [ ] _____
- [ ] _____
- [ ] _____
- [ ] _____

- [ ] _____
- [ ] _____
- [ ] _____
- [ ] _____
- [ ] _____
- [ ] _____
- [ ] _____
- [ ] _____
- [ ] _____
- [ ] _____
- [ ] _____
- [ ] _____
- [ ] _____
- [ ] _____
- [ ] _____
- [ ] _____
- [ ] _____

Bachelor Party Notes

Bachelor Party Menu

Menu

Snacks & Appetizers:

_____

_____

_____

_____

_____

_____

Main Food:

_____

_____

_____

_____

_____

_____

_____

Grocery list

☐ _____

☐ _____

☐ _____

☐ _____

☐ _____

☐ _____

☐ _____

☐ _____

☐ _____

☐ _____

☐ _____

☐ _____

☐ _____

☐ _____

☐ _____

☐ _____

☐ _____

☐ _____

☐ _____

☐ _____

Bachelor Party Menu

Drinks:

_____

_____

_____

_____

_____

_____

Cake:

_____

_____

_____

☐ _____

☐ _____

☐ _____

☐ _____

☐ _____

☐ _____

☐ _____

☐ _____

☐ _____

☐ _____

☐ _____

☐ _____

☐ _____

Notes:

_____

_____

_____

_____

Bachelor Party Expenses

Food / Drinks	Budgeted Amt.	Amt. Spent	Notes
Total			
Supplies			
Total			
Entertainment			
Total			

Rehearsal Dinner Planner

Rehearsal Dinner Planner

Date and Time _____

Venue _____   Contact Person _____

Website _____   Phone #1 _____

Phone #2 _____   Email _____

Address _____

Theme _____

Flowers & Decor   Shopping list

_____   ☐ _____

_____   ☐ _____

_____   ☐ _____

Food & Drinks   ☐ _____

_____   ☐ _____

_____   ☐ _____

_____   ☐ _____

                                       ☐ _____

Favors   ☐ _____

_____   ☐ _____

_____   ☐ _____

_____   ☐ _____

_____   ☐ _____

                                       ☐ _____

Rehearsal Dinner List

Date and Time

Guest Name	Email	RSVP	Food / Beverages Brought

Rehearsal Dinner Schedule

Time	Task or Activity	Notes

Rehearsal Dinner Gift Tracker

Gift	Gift Description	Gift By	Thank -You Card Sent?
			☐
			☐
			☐
			☐
			☐
			☐
			☐
			☐
			☐
			☐
			☐
			☐
			☐
			☐
			☐
			☐
			☐
			☐
			☐
			☐
			☐
			☐
			☐
			☐
			☐
			☐
			☐
			☐

Rehearsal Dinner Timeline

When ?	To-Do	Notes	Done
			☐
			☐
			☐
			☐
			☐
			☐
			☐
			☐
			☐
			☐
			☐
			☐
			☐
			☐
			☐
			☐
			☐
			☐
			☐
			☐
			☐
			☐
			☐
			☐
			☐
			☐
			☐
			☐

Rehearsal Dinner Shopping List

- [ ] _____
- [ ] _____
- [ ] _____
- [ ] _____
- [ ] _____
- [ ] _____
- [ ] _____
- [ ] _____
- [ ] _____
- [ ] _____
- [ ] _____
- [ ] _____
- [ ] _____
- [ ] _____
- [ ] _____
- [ ] _____
- [ ] _____
- [ ] _____

- [ ] _____
- [ ] _____
- [ ] _____
- [ ] _____
- [ ] _____
- [ ] _____
- [ ] _____
- [ ] _____
- [ ] _____
- [ ] _____
- [ ] _____
- [ ] _____
- [ ] _____
- [ ] _____
- [ ] _____
- [ ] _____
- [ ] _____
- [ ] _____

Rehearsal Dinner Notes

Rehearsal Dinner Party Menu

Menu

Snacks & Appetizers:

_____

_____

_____

_____

_____

_____

_____

Main Food:

_____

_____

_____

_____

_____

_____

_____

Grocery list

☐ _____

☐ _____

☐ _____

☐ _____

☐ _____

☐ _____

☐ _____

☐ _____

☐ _____

☐ _____

☐ _____

☐ _____

☐ _____

☐ _____

☐ _____

☐ _____

☐ _____

☐ _____

☐ _____

Rehearsal Dinner Party Menu

Drinks:

_____   ☐ _____
_____   ☐ _____
_____   ☐ _____
_____   ☐ _____
_____   ☐ _____
_____   ☐ _____
_____   ☐ _____
_____   ☐ _____
_____   ☐ _____

Cake:
                             ☐ _____
_____   ☐ _____
_____   ☐ _____
_____   ☐ _____
_____   ☐ _____

Notes:

_____

_____

_____

_____

Rehearsal Dinner Expenses

Food / Drinks	Budgeted Amt.	Amt. Spent	Notes
Total			
Supplies			
Total			
Entertainment			
Total			

Suppiler Planner

The Florist

Company : _____

Contact Person : _____ Phone : _____

Email : _____

Contact On the Day : _____ Phone : _____

Email : _____

Service Overview

_____
_____
_____

Supplier Service Datial

_____
_____
_____
_____
_____

Notes

_____
_____
_____
_____

The Cake Maker

Company : _____

Contact Person : _____ Phone : _____

Email : _____

Contact On the Day : _____ Phone : _____

Email : _____

Service Overview
_____
_____
_____

Supplier Service Datial
_____
_____
_____
_____
_____

Notes
_____
_____
_____
_____

The Officiant

Company : _____

Contact Person : _____ Phone : _____

Email : _____

Contact On the Day : _____ Phone : _____

Email : _____

Service Overview

_____
_____

Supplier Service Datial

_____
_____
_____
_____
_____

Notes

_____
_____
_____
_____

The Music

Company : _____

Contact Person : _____ Phone : _____

Email : _____

Contact On the Day : _____ Phone : _____

Email : _____

Service Overview

_____
_____

Supplier Service Datial

_____
_____
_____
_____
_____

Notes

_____
_____
_____
_____

The Photographer

Company : _____

Contact Person : _____ Phone : _____

Email : _____

Contact On the Day : _____ Phone : _____

Email : _____

Service Overview

_____
_____

Supplier Service Datial

_____
_____
_____
_____
_____

Notes

_____
_____
_____
_____

The Videographer

Company : _____

Contact Person : _____ Phone : _____

Email : _____

Contact On the Day : _____ Phone : _____

Email : _____

Service Overview

_____
_____

Supplier Service Datial

_____
_____
_____
_____
_____

Notes

_____
_____
_____
_____

The Designer

Company : _____

Contact Person : _____ Phone : _____

Email : _____

Contact On the Day : _____ Phone : _____

Email : _____

Service Overview

_____

_____

Supplier Service Datial

_____

_____

_____

_____

Notes

_____

_____

_____

_____

The Stationery Designer

Company : _____

Contact Person :_____ Phone : _____

Email : _____

Contact On the Day : _____ Phone : _____

Email : _____

Service Overview

_____
_____

Supplier Service Datial

_____
_____
_____
_____
_____

Notes

_____
_____
_____

Daily Planner

Date : _____

5.00 A.M. _____	5.00 P.M. _____
5.30 A.M. _____	5.30 P.M. _____
6.30 A.M. _____	6.00 P.M. _____
7.00 A.M. _____	6.30 P.M. _____
7.30 A.M. _____	7.00 P.M. _____
8.00 A.M. _____	7.30 P.M. _____
8.30 A.M. _____	8.00 P.M. _____
9.00 A.M. _____	8.30 P.M. _____
9.30 A.M. _____	9.00 P.M. _____
10.00 A.M. _____	9.30 P.M. _____
10.30 A.M. _____	10.00 P.M. _____
11.00 A.M. _____	10.30 P.M. _____
11.30 A.M. _____	11.00 P.M. _____
12.00 P.M. _____	11.30 P.M. _____
12.30 P.M. _____	12.00 P.M. _____
1.00 P.M. _____	12.30 P.M. _____
1.30 P.M. _____	1.00 A.M. _____
2.00 P.M. _____	2.00 A.M. _____
2.30 P.M. _____	3.00 A.M. _____
3.00 P.M. _____	4.00 A.M. _____
3.30 P.M. _____	Notes
4.00 P.M. _____	_____

Week of: _____

Sunday

- [ ]
- [ ]
- [ ]
- [ ]
- [ ]
- [ ]

Monday

- [ ]
- [ ]
- [ ]
- [ ]
- [ ]
- [ ]

Tuesday

- [ ]
- [ ]
- [ ]
- [ ]
- [ ]
- [ ]

Wednesday

- [ ]
- [ ]
- [ ]
- [ ]
- [ ]
- [ ]

Thursday

- [ ]
- [ ]
- [ ]
- [ ]
- [ ]
- [ ]

Friday

- [ ]
- [ ]
- [ ]
- [ ]
- [ ]
- [ ]

Saturday

- [ ]
- [ ]
- [ ]
- [ ]
- [ ]
- [ ]

Notes

- [ ]
- [ ]
- [ ]
- [ ]
- [ ]
- [ ]

Week of: _____

Sunday
- [ ]
- [ ]
- [ ]
- [ ]
- [ ]
- [ ]

Monday
- [ ]
- [ ]
- [ ]
- [ ]
- [ ]
- [ ]

Tuesday
- [ ]
- [ ]
- [ ]
- [ ]
- [ ]
- [ ]

Wednesday
- [ ]
- [ ]
- [ ]
- [ ]
- [ ]
- [ ]

Thursday
- [ ]
- [ ]
- [ ]
- [ ]
- [ ]
- [ ]

Friday
- [ ]
- [ ]
- [ ]
- [ ]
- [ ]
- [ ]

Saturday
- [ ]
- [ ]
- [ ]
- [ ]
- [ ]
- [ ]

Notes
- [ ]
- [ ]
- [ ]
- [ ]
- [ ]
- [ ]

Monthly Planner

Monday	Tuesday	Wednesday	Thrusday

Monthly Planner

Month Of : _____

Friday	Satruday	Sunday	To Do List

Notes :
_____
_____
_____

Monthly Planner

Monday	Tuesday	Wednesday	Thrusday

Monthly Planner

Month Of : _____

Friday	Satruday	Sunday	To Do List
			☐ _____
			☐ _____
			☐ _____
			☐ _____
			☐ _____
			☐ _____
			☐ _____
			☐ _____
			☐ _____
			☐ _____
			☐ _____
			☐ _____
			☐ _____
			☐ _____
			☐ _____
			☐ _____
			☐ _____

Notes :

_____

_____

_____

Yearly Planner

Year : _____

January

- [ ]
- [ ]
- [ ]
- [ ]
- [ ]
- [ ]
- [ ]

Febuary

- [ ]
- [ ]
- [ ]
- [ ]
- [ ]
- [ ]
- [ ]

March

- [ ]
- [ ]
- [ ]
- [ ]
- [ ]
- [ ]
- [ ]

April

- [ ]
- [ ]
- [ ]
- [ ]
- [ ]
- [ ]
- [ ]

May

- [ ]
- [ ]
- [ ]
- [ ]
- [ ]
- [ ]
- [ ]

June

- [ ]
- [ ]
- [ ]
- [ ]
- [ ]
- [ ]
- [ ]

Yearly Planner

July

- [ ]
- [ ]
- [ ]
- [ ]
- [ ]
- [ ]
- [ ]

August

- [ ]
- [ ]
- [ ]
- [ ]
- [ ]
- [ ]
- [ ]

September

- [ ]
- [ ]
- [ ]
- [ ]
- [ ]
- [ ]
- [ ]

October

- [ ]
- [ ]
- [ ]
- [ ]
- [ ]
- [ ]
- [ ]

November

- [ ]
- [ ]
- [ ]
- [ ]
- [ ]
- [ ]
- [ ]

December

- [ ]
- [ ]
- [ ]
- [ ]
- [ ]
- [ ]
- [ ]

Monthly Wedding Checklist

12 months before

- Announce the engagement to family and friends
- Arrange a family meeting
- Set the date
- Start planning the guest list
- Contact bridesmaids
- Purchase a wedding planner/binder
- Decided on a budget and determine who is paying for what
- Reserve ceremony site
- Book vendors: photographer / videographer, church / officiant, caterer, florist,Venue, baker, band, and DJ.
- Start shopping for wedding dresses
- Book hotel rooms for out of town guests
- Research suppliers
- Sort wedding license
- Create an inspiration board on Pinterest
- Decide a wedding theme, style and formality
- Contact wedding planners / consultants (if you decided to use one)
- Engagement party
- Reserve reception site
- Register the engagement gifts
- Order thank-you notes for engagement gifts
- Create a wedding website
-
-

Monthly Wedding Checklist

10 months before

- Start your wedding fitness and diet plan (set realistic goals)
- Make bridal salon appointments
- Order and mail save the date cards
- Shop for bridal party gifts
- Meet with your favorite caterers
- Purchase dress and have the necessary alterations done
- Finalize guest list
- Choose music for the ceremony and reception
- Choose decor for ceremony and reception
- Taste cakes and order wedding cake
- Register for the gifts
- Decide on bridesmaids' dresses
- Shop for wedding stationery
- Purchase wedding bands
- Start planning the honeymoon
- Have engagement photos taken
- Look into grooms' attire
- Order accessories and jewelry
- Arrange transportation for grooms and guests
-
-
-
-
-
-

Monthly Wedding Checklist

6 months before

- Finalize details with all vendors
- Shop for bridesmaids dresses
- Start choosing the playlist and do not playlist
- Select first dance and other special dance songs
- Attend dance lessons
- Make arrangements for rental items
- Make necessary alterations for groom's attire
- Book accommodations for the wedding night
- Design and order wedding invitations
-
-
-

4 months before

- Plan a bridal shower
- Buy wedding rings
- Attend necessary wedding counseling sessions with the officiant
- Schedule the bridal party
- Schedule wedding rehearsal with officiant
- Buy wedding rings
- Purchase a guest book
-
-
-
-

Monthly Wedding Checklist

3 months before

- Mail wedding invitations
- Order favors
- Discuss finalize flowers arrangements for reception and ceremony
- Plan the order of the ceremony
- Discuss finalized menu options and costs with caterer
- Order invitations for rehearsal dinner
-
-
-
-

2 months before

- Attend bridal shower
- Write thank-you notes for the bridal shower and mail them
- Start writing on your wedding vows
- Schedule fitting for the flower girls and bridesmaids
- Make a reception timeline
- Order wedding programs
- Send a shot list to your videographer and photographer
- Buy lingerie
- Contact all those who haven't RSVP'd
-
-

Monthly Wedding Checklist

1 month before

- Get marriage license
- Mail invitations for the rehearsal dinner
- Start seating arrangements
- Purchase gift for your bridesmaids'
- Finish writing your vows
- Have a final dress fitting
- Review music list with your musician or DJ
- Finalize details with wedding service providers
- Order alcohol and beverages
-
-
-

2 weeks before

- Organize wedding-day attire
- Confirm rehearsal plans
- Pick up wedding license
- Give a final head count to the caterer
- Complete seating plan
- Confirm date, time and other details with all vendors
- Pick up dress
- Confirm honeymoon reservations
- Create a wedding day schedule
-
-

Monthly Wedding Checklist

1 week before

- Have groom and groomsmen pick-up their suits/tuxedos
- Distribute wedding day timeline to vendors
- Confirm wedding day details with all vendors
- Set aside tips for vendors
- Pack for your honeymoon
- Break in your shoes
- Have a pre-wedding beauty treatments
-
-
-

1 day before

- Get a manicure and pedicure
- Pack wedding emergency kit
- Attend rehearsal and rehearsal dinner
- Give thank you gifts to attendants
- Get an early night
- Put wedding attires and accessories together
- Practice vows
-
-
-
-

Top 25 Romantic First Dance Songs

1   Rent "I'll Cover You"
2   Lonestar "Amazed"
3   Bright Eyes "This Is the First Day of My Life"
4   Frankie Valli or Lauryn Hill "Can't Take My Eyes Off of You"
5   The Beatles "In My Life"
6   Rilo Kiley "I Never"
7   Train "Marry Me"
8   The Rolling Stones "Wild Horses"
9   Bruno Mars "Marry You"
10   Nat King Cole "Unforgettable"
11   Snow Patrol " Chasing Cars"
12   Sade "By Your Side"
13   Stevie Wonder "For Once In My Life"
14   Jack Johnson "Better Together"
15   Frank Sinatra "Fly Me to the Moon"
16   Elvis Presley "Falling in Love with You"
17   She & Him "I Was Made For You"
18   Paolo Nutini "Loving You"
19   Loving You "All of Me"
20   Adele "Make You Feel My Love"
21   Beyonce "Love on Top"
22   The Cure "Friday I'm In Love"
23   Elton John "Your Song"
24   Ben E. King "Stand by Me"
25   Alison Krauss ft. Union Station "When You Say Nothing at All"

The Hair Appointment

Hair Stylist Name: _____

Salon _____ Phone # _____

Email _____ Website _____

Address _____

Trial Appointment

Date _____ Time _____

Trial Fee _____ Tip _____

Notes _____

_____

Wedding Day Appointment

Date _____ Time _____

Cost _____ Tip _____

Location _____

Estimated Number Of Hours _____

Hair trial Photos

The Maker Appointment

Markup Stylist Name: _____

Salon _____   Phone # _____

Email _____   Website _____

Address _____

Trial Appointment

Date _____   Time _____

Trial Fee _____   Tip _____

Notes _____

_____

Wedding Day Appointment

Date _____   Time _____

Cost _____   Tip _____

Location _____

Estimated Number Of Hours _____

Markup trial Photos

The Ceremony Worksheet

Company Name: _____

Contact Person _____ Phone # _____

Email _____ Website _____

Address _____

Notes _____

_____

_____

_____

_____

_____

_____

_____

_____

_____

_____

_____

_____

_____

_____

_____

_____

The Emergency Kits

For the bride

- [ ] pain killers
- [ ] lip balm
- [ ] clear nail polish
- [ ] colored nail polish
- [ ] super glue
- [ ] stain remover
- [ ] q-tips
- [ ] elastic bands
- [ ] deodorant
- [ ] perfume
- [ ] phone charger
- [ ] contact lenses
- [ ] flats
- [ ] breath mints
- [ ] small scissors
- [ ] baby powder
- [ ] toothbrush
- [ ] eyeliner
- [ ] toothpaste
- [ ] safety pins
- [ ] eyeshadow
- [ ] hairspray
- [ ] sewing kit
- [ ] brush
- [ ] fashion tape

For the groom

- [ ] pain killers
- [ ] deodorant
- [ ] q-tips
- [ ] extra pair of shoelaces
- [ ] lip balm
- [ ] brush
- [ ] hairspray
- [ ] band-aids
- [ ] hair gel
- [ ] stain remover
- [ ] sewing kit
- [ ] cologne
- [ ] extra socks
- [ ] contact lenses
- [ ] contact solution
- [ ] eye drops
- [ ] small snack
- [ ] phone charger
- [ ] toothbrush
- [ ] toothpaste
- [ ] mouthwash
- [ ] dental floss
- [ ] safety pins
- [ ] tissues
- [ ] shoe polish kit

The Emergency Kits

For the bride

- ☐ _____
- ☐ _____
- ☐ _____
- ☐ _____
- ☐ _____
- ☐ _____
- ☐ _____
- ☐ _____
- ☐ _____
- ☐ _____
- ☐ _____
- ☐ _____
- ☐ _____
- ☐ _____
- ☐ _____
- ☐ _____
- ☐ _____
- ☐ _____
- ☐ _____
- ☐ _____

For the groom

- ☐ _____
- ☐ _____
- ☐ _____
- ☐ _____
- ☐ _____
- ☐ _____
- ☐ _____
- ☐ _____
- ☐ _____
- ☐ _____
- ☐ _____
- ☐ _____
- ☐ _____
- ☐ _____
- ☐ _____
- ☐ _____
- ☐ _____
- ☐ _____
- ☐ _____
- ☐ _____

The Playlist

Song suggestions

Do not play

Wedding Music

Ceremony

Guest Arrival / Prelude _____

Processional Music _____

Ceremony Music _____

Recessional _____

Guest Depart _____

Reception

Announcement Song _____

Bridesmaids _____

Groomsmen _____

Maid Of Honor _____

Best Man _____

Bride and Groom's Entrance _____

First Dance _____

Mother and Son Dance _____

Father and Daughter Dance _____

Guests First Dance _____

Traditional Dance _____

Grandparents Dance _____

Bouquet Toss _____

Cake Cutting _____

Garter Toss _____

Maid Of Honor Toast _____

Best Man Toast _____

Closing Song _____

The Registry Worksheet

Store _____   Store Hours _____

Contact Person _____   Phone # _____

Website _____   Email _____

Address _____

Notes _____

Store _____   Store Hours _____

Contact Person _____   Phone # _____

Website _____   Email _____

Address _____

Notes _____

Store _____   Store Hours _____

Contact Person _____   Phone # _____

Website _____   Email _____

Address _____

Notes _____

Store _____   Store Hours _____

Contact Person _____   Phone # _____

Website _____   Email _____

Address _____

Notes _____

The Wedding

Maid of honor

Name : _____

Phone : _____

Email : _____

Special Assignments : _____

_____

_____

Bridesmaid 1

Name : _____

Phone : _____

Email : _____

Special Assignments : _____

_____

_____

Bridesmaid 2

Name : _____

Phone : _____

Email : _____

Special Assignments : _____

_____

_____

Bridesmaid 3

Name : _____

Phone : _____

Email : _____

Special Assignments : _____

_____

_____

Bridesmaid 4

Name : _____

Phone : _____

Email : _____

Special Assignments : _____

_____

_____

Flower girl

Name : _____

Parents Name : _____

Parents Phone : _____

Email : _____

Special Assignments : _____

_____

The Wedding

Best man

Name : _____

Phone : _____

Email : _____

Special Assignments : _____

_____

Groomsman 1

Name : _____

Phone : _____

Email : _____

Special Assignments : _____

_____

Groomsman 2

Name : _____

Phone : _____

Email : _____

Special Assignments : _____

_____

Groomsman 3

Name : _____

Phone : _____

Email : _____

Special Assignments : _____

_____

Groomsman 4

Name : _____

Phone : _____

Email : _____

Special Assignments : _____

_____

Ring bearer

Name : _____

Parents Name: _____

Parents Phon : _____

Email : _____

Special Assignments : _____

_____

Drinks List

White wine

_____

_____

_____

_____

Champagne

_____

_____

_____

_____

Whiskey

_____

_____

_____

Cocktails

_____

_____

_____

Red wine

_____

_____

_____

_____

Blush wine

_____

_____

_____

_____

Liquor

_____

_____

_____

Other

_____

_____

_____

The Rings

Store _____

Jeweler _____ Phone # _____

Email _____ Website _____

Address _____

Wedding ring inscriptions

Brides' Inscription: _____

_____

Grooms' Inscription: _____

_____

_____

Budget

Item	Budgeted Amt	Actual Amt	Difference
Bride's Ring			
Groom's Ring			
Bride's Ring Fitting			
Groom's Ring Fitting			

Notes : _____

_____

_____

Gift Registry Organizer

Gift	Gift By	Thank-You Card Sent?	Notes
		☐	
		☐	
		☐	
		☐	
		☐	
		☐	
		☐	
		☐	
		☐	
		☐	
		☐	
		☐	
		☐	
		☐	
		☐	
		☐	
		☐	
		☐	
		☐	
		☐	
		☐	
		☐	
		☐	
		☐	
		☐	
		☐	
		☐	
		☐	
		☐	

Caterer Comparison

Caterer 1

Contact Person

Address

Phone #

Website

Email

Caterer 2

Contact Person

Address

Phone #

Website

Email

Caterer 3

Contact Person

Address

Phone #

Website

Email

Caterer 4

Contact Person

Address

Phone #

Website

Email

Cost Of	Caterer 1	Caterer 2	Caterer 3	Caterer 4
Desserts				
Allergen Alternatives				
Dinner				
Brunch				
Buffet				
Seasonal Food				

Questions For Your Caterer

Caterer _____

All inclusive rate ?

Rate per plate ?

Does he have a license ?

Meals will be prepared from scratch?

Does he provide the chairs, linens and silverware?

Does he cater other weddings that day? How many?

Does he offer event packages?

Does he do wedding cakes?

What does he do with leftovers?

Can he accommodate dietary restrictions?

What brands of alcohol will be served?

Will we receive a written contract?

What is the serve-to-guest ratio?

How much he charges for children's meals?

Will he provide a wait staff?

What will they wear?

Does he charge a cake cutting fee?

When does he need a final guest count?

Can he provide reference from previous clients?

Do we need to handle the bar separately or does he provide alcohol?

What are his overtime fees?

Is there an extra charge for food tasting?

What services are not included?

Videography

Company Name: _____

Contact Person _____ Phone # _____

Email _____

Contact On The Day: _____ Phone # _____

Email _____

Service Overview / Style _____

_____

_____

People To Be Sure To Include

1.	5
2	6
3	7
4	8

Item / Service	Cost
Videography	
Video Edits	
DVDs	
Total	

Menu Ideas

Desserts

_____
_____
_____
_____

Appetizers

_____
_____
_____
_____

Main

_____
_____
_____
_____

Drinks

_____
_____
_____
_____

Notes

_____
_____
_____
_____
_____
_____

Vows

_____
_____
_____
_____
_____
_____
_____
_____
_____
_____
_____
_____
_____
_____
_____
_____
_____
_____
_____
_____

Transportation

Transportation Company
_____

Address
_____

Contact Person   Phone #
_____

Email
_____

Notes
_____

_____

Car 1

Model   Driver's Name
_____

Phone #
_____

Notes
_____

Car 2

Model   Driver's Name
_____

Phone #
_____

Notes
_____

Car 3

Model   Driver's Name
_____

Phone #
_____

Notes
_____

Transportation

Car	Capacity	Pickup Location	Pickup Time	Cost/Hr	Est. Hrs	Cost
Total						

Guest Transportation

Car	Guest	Pickup Location	Pickup Time

Seating Arrangements

1. _____
2. _____
3. _____
4. _____
5. _____
6. _____
7. _____
8. _____

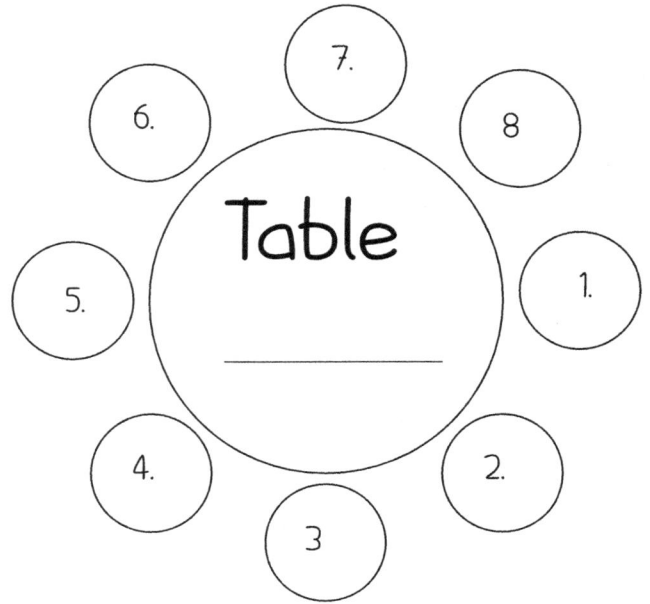

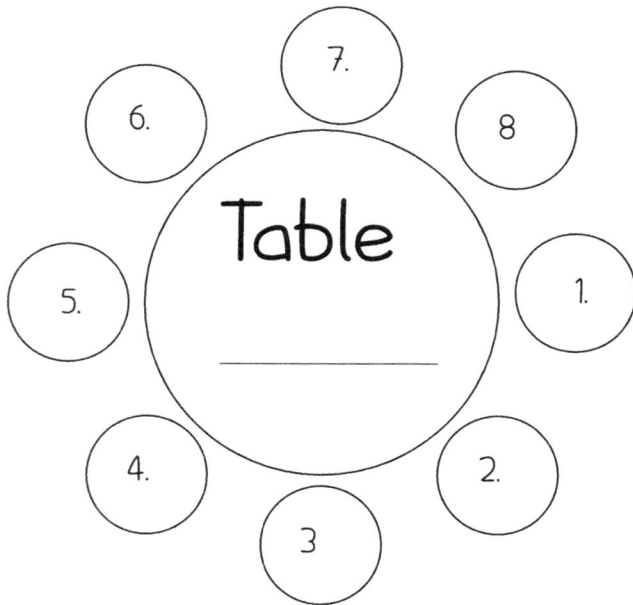

1. _____
2. _____
3. _____
4. _____
5. _____
6. _____
7. _____
8. _____

Seating Arrangements - Head Table

Kitchen

Bridal Table

Band or DJ

Cake

Groom's Parents

Bridl's Parents

Guests

Guests

Guests

Dance Floor

Guests

Guests

Guests

Guests

Place Cards

Gift Table

Guest Parking

Wedding Photos

The Gift Registry

Item	Website / Store	Received ?
		☐
		☐
		☐
		☐
		☐
		☐
		☐
		☐
		☐
		☐
		☐
		☐
		☐
		☐
		☐
		☐
		☐
		☐
		☐
		☐
		☐
		☐
		☐
		☐
		☐
		☐
		☐

Quotes For Wedding Toasts

"Love never gives up, never loses faith, is always hopeful and endures through every circumstance." – 1 Corinthians 13:7

"May you grow old on one pillow." – Armenian blessing

"Love is blind – marriage is the eye-opener." – Pauline Thomason

"Laughter is the shortest distance between two people."
– Victor Borge

"Marriage is like a golden ring in a chain, whose beginning is a glance and whose ending is eternity." – Kahlil Gibran

"Love is a moment that lasts forever." – Anonymous

"In our life there is a single color, as on an artist's palette, which provides the meaning of life and art. It is the color of love."
– Marc Chagall

"There is only one happiness in life, to love and be loved."
– George Sand

"I love you very much, probably more than anybody could love another person."
– 50 First Dates

"Love does not consist of gazing at each other, but in looking outward together in the same direction." – Antoine de Saint-Exupéry

"Love is a symbol of eternity. It wipes out all sense of time, destroying all memory of a beginning and all fear of an end."
– Anonymous

"Don't marry the person you think you can live with; marry only the individual you think you can't live without." – James C. Dobson

"May your love be like the misty rain, gentle coming in but flooding the river."
– Traditional African

Venue Comparison

Venue 1

Contact Person _____

Address _____

Phone # _____

Website _____

Email _____

Capacity _____

Venue 2

Contact Person _____

Address _____

Phone # _____

Website _____

Email _____

Capacity _____

Venue 3

Contact Person _____

Address _____

Phone # _____

Website _____

Email _____

Capacity _____

Venue 4

Contact Person _____

Address _____

Phone # _____

Website _____

Email _____

Capacity _____

Cost Of	Venue 1	Venue 2	Venue 3	Venue 4
Rental Fee				
Parking Lots Available				
Decor				
Cancellation Cost				
Deposit Schedule				
Capacity				

Questions To Ask Each Venue

Venue _____

Available dates ?

How many guests can accommodate ?

What's the fee? What does that include ?

Can this venue accommodate a DJ or band ?

How much is the deposit and when is it due ?

What's the payment plan ?

Do they provide a coat check service ?

Is VAT included in price ?

How many restrooms are there ?

Is there room for dancing ?

Are they hosting any other weddings at the same time as ours?

Will the guests have to pay for parking ?

Can we bring our own alcohol ?

Is the venue handicap accessible ?

Do they have a liquor license ?

What is the seating arrangement ?

How many hours do they allow a party to be there?

What type of tables do they have?

Do you have an on-site venue coordinator ?

If the venue is outdoor, what is the backup plan in case of rain ?

Where can we store wedding gifts ?

How long we have to clean up ?

Do they offer a discount for off-season dates ?

Is there an in-house caterer ? Do we have to use him ?

Questions To Ask Each Venue

Venue _____

_____
_____
_____
_____
_____
_____
_____
_____
_____
_____
_____
_____
_____
_____
_____
_____
_____
_____
_____
_____
_____
_____

Decorations

Decorator: _____

Address _____

Phone # _____ Email _____

Website _____ Cost _____

Package_____

Ceremony

Item	Description
Pew Ends	
Aisle	
Altar	
Entrance Wreath	
Flower Girl	

Reception

Item	Description
Entrance	
Bar Decorations	
Car Decorations	
Centerpieces	
Gift Table	
Cake Table	
Head Table	
Chairs	

Vendor Payment Plan

Ceremony

Company	Item	Deposit	Deposit Due	Total	Diff Due Date

Reception

Company	Item	Deposit	Deposit Due	Total	Diff Due Date

Rental Worksheet

Rental Company _____

Address _____

Contact Person _____ Phone # _____

Website _____ Email _____

Notes _____

_____

Rental items

Item	Qty.	Details

Questions For Your Caterer

Caterer _____

_____

_____

_____

_____

_____

_____

_____

_____

_____

_____

_____

_____

_____

_____

_____

_____

_____

_____

_____

_____

_____

Questions For Your Photographer

Photographer/Videographer _____

Are you available on our wedding day?

Is photography your full time job ?

How many weddings will you be working on that day / weekend ?

How long will you stay at our wedding ?

How long have you been photographing weddings ?

Can we see a list of reviews and samples of your work ?

Will you provide a contract for your services ?

How much of a deposit do you require ? When is it due ?

Do you offer a payment plan ?

What happens if an emergency occurs and you can't photograph my wedding?

Will you edit and color correct my images ?

What attire will the photographers be wearing ?

Do you have insurance ?

Have you ever worked on our location before ?

What style do you specialize in ?

What exactly is included in your packages ?

Can we see the album from a recent full wedding ?

When can we expect to see the photos after the wedding ?

Are you willing to follow a shot list ?

What type of paper will you use for the album and prints ?

Are you the photographer that will shoot our wedding?

Will you have any assistants on our wedding day ?

What's your refund policy ?

If the event lasts longer are you willing to stay ? Do you charge extra ?

Do you work with a videography team ?

Questions For Your Photographer

Photographer/Videographer _____

_____

_____

_____

_____

_____

_____

_____

_____

_____

_____

_____

_____

_____

_____

_____

_____

_____

_____

_____

_____

_____

_____

Notes

Notes

Notes

Notes

Notes

Notes

Notes

Notes

Notes

Notes

Notes

Made in the USA
Las Vegas, NV
09 June 2022